THE FORGOTTEN
BIBLE READING METHOD

*HOW TO READ AND UNDERSTAND THE BIBLE
IN 5 SIMPLE STEPS*

WAYNE DAVIES

Get free Bible reading tips at
www.GodWroteTheBook.com

This book was previously published as
God Wrote The Book: Do You Know How To Read It?

Open my eyes that I may see
wonderful things in your law.
Psalm 119:18

What People Are Saying About This Book

Loved this book! I am going to put these principles into practice right away! This is a small book that you can read in one night and it is packed with valuable information on how to know God more through the reading of the Scriptures. It's a fresh new look at an old way of studying the Word. Would recommend this book to anyone who struggles with reading God's Word!
-- *Douglas J. Van Weide*

There are thousands of books about the Bible and the average American Christian apparently loves to read about the Bible, various explanations on what it means, even novels written about biblical characters. Many of these books about the Bible even make the bestseller lists. Certainly some of those books have a place in our learning process. However, what many, if not most, American Christians don't do is actually read the Bible!

Wayne's passion and desire is for Christians to actually READ the Bible. His self-proclaimed description of his book is found in the first line of his introduction: "This is a book about a book about The Book." So why should we read this book about the Bible? Because here he gives us a practical method to ACTUALLY READ the Bible. A method first published in 1904 and one that has been used by many pastors and teachers of our day. If you are ready to really dig into God's Word, this is a book that will help you to do exactly that. To God be the glory! *-- Stan Helpler*

The Bible is God's love letter to us, but sometimes we do not completely understand how he is presenting His love. Wayne has been inspired by God to write a guide for us to more fully understand what God is saying to us. God has commanded us to base our life on the Word of God. "This book of the law shall not depart from your mouth, but you shall meditate on it day and night, so that you may be careful to do all that is written in it. For then you will make your way prosperous, and then you will have good success" (Joshua 1: 8). Wayne's book will show you how to keep God's command.
-- Margaret Reese

A real helpful little book. I think a lot of us have this nagging feeling at times that the early Christians had each letter by Paul, for example, read to them in one reading and had a good idea what the author was trying to tell them. We need to begin where they began, reading each book or letter at least, in one sitting. Thanks to Wayne for a good common sense approach to Bible study.
-- Graham Rogers

FREE GIFTS

As my way of saying "Thank You" for reading this book, I have two special gifts for you.

GIFT #1

If you are looking for more Bible reading tips, I've put together a Resource Guide entitled, "Top 5 Free Online Bible Study Tools".

You can get your free copy at www.GodWroteTheBook.com

These resources will provide the tools you need to read and study the Bible with greater understanding and Christ-honoring, life-changing results! Enjoy!

GIFT #2

When you sign up for the Resource Guide, you'll also receive a free subscription to my online Bible study newsletter. Bible reading tips will be delivered to your inbox every week.

And may God continue to enrich your life for His glory as you spend time with Him in the Word.

Grace & Peace,
Wayne Davies

TABLE OF CONTENTS

WHY I WROTE THIS BOOK

When it comes to Bible reading, it seems to me that the amount of time Christians spend actually reading and studying the Scriptures varies greatly. I know believers who spend hours every day in the Word. And I know believers who spend little if any time at all in the Word.

Perhaps I shouldn't be surprised. I am concerned, however, about those who profess to know Christ yet spend so little time listening to what he has to say. I've become acutely aware that the average Christian has become increasingly and sadly biblically illiterate.

I can think of at least two reasons for this.

REASON #1

Could it be that some Christians have forgotten to read the Bible? We have filled our lives with many worthwhile activities both inside and outside the local church building. We spend hours helping people in any number of ways – both locally and worldwide.

We engage in many acts of kindness, random and intentional. We help our neighbor across the street and on the other side of the globe. And this outpouring of love is a good thing, especially when done in the name of Jesus and for the glory of Jesus.

When I look around at the Christians I associate with, I see people doing wonderful things for others. I see Christians living out Galatians 6:10 – "Therefore, as we have opportunity, let us do good to all people, especially to those who belong to the family of believers."

We like to be busy helping others. I find no fault with that. Amen?

But when was the last time you met with a group of Christians and simply read and listened to the Bible?

In my local church, not long ago, a Sunday morning worship service was devoted to the reading of God's Word. In lieu of the sermon, anyone who had memorized a psalm was allowed to stand up and recite it from memory or read it.

When I first heard about this, I wondered how it would play out. How many people would have the courage to read or recite a Scripture passage in front of the entire church?

My fears were unfounded as this worship service turned out to be pure delight. I didn't count how many people stood up and read a psalm (most did it from memory), but people kept getting up, one after another, and it lasted for at least 30 minutes. It was awesome!

I love the psalms. Over the past 10 years I've cultivated the habit of reading through the Psalms, one each day, when I first wake up in the morning. This is how I start my daily time in the Word and prayer.

So it was thrilling to sit there and listen to the reading of holy Scripture for 30 truth-filled, glory-packed minutes. I was so excited at how well it went. And I remember thinking, "This is such a easy thing to do. No music. No fanfare. No drama. Just God's people reading and hearing God's Word."

I went home greatly encouraged. My motivation to spend more time reading the Bible went up a few notches. Oh, how God loves for us to be still and open our ears to hear him speak!

How about you? Does spending time in the Word thrill your soul and satisfy your longing to be in the presence of our Creator and Sustainer?

How are you doing in this area of your Christian walk? Do you set aside time regularly, even daily, to feed on God's truth? "Man does not live on bread alone, but on every word that comes from the mouth of God" (Matthew 4:4).

Luke recorded a marvelous account of Jesus and two sisters, Martha and Mary.

"As Jesus and his disciples were on their way, he came to a village where a woman named Martha opened her home to him. She had a sister called Mary, who sat at the Lord's feet listening to what he said. But Martha was distracted by all the preparations that had to be made. She came to him and asked, 'Lord, don't you care that my sister has left me to do the work by myself? Tell her to help me!'

'Martha, Martha,' the Lord answered, 'you are worried and upset about many things, but few things are needed—or indeed only one. Mary has chosen what is better, and it will

not   be   taken   away   from   her.'"
Luke 10:38-42

There is so much truth in this passage, but let me draw your attention to two things that jump off the page and into my heart. What did Mary like to do? She "sat at the feet of Jesus listening to what he said." Isn't that wonderful?

And what did Jesus say about this? "Mary has chosen what is better." Wow! What a commendation from the lips of our Lord.

Reality Check: Whom do you identify with in this story? Mary or Martha? What would you rather do, spend time at the feet of Jesus, listening to His Word, or checking off a few things on your To Do List?

When you have time to yourself, what do you do? Surf the Internet. Catch up with friends on Facebook. Talk on the phone. Watch TV (my own Achilles heel and #1 time waster).

How much time do you spend reading the Bible, sitting at the feet of Jesus, enthralled with him, amazed by him, worshipping him while he speaks to you?

This preoccupation with doing things other than listening to God is of great concern to me. And so my hope is that this book will challenge you to take a close look at your own life and how you spend your time.

My prayer is that this book will provide the motivation and the means to spend more time sitting at the feet of Jesus by reading the Bible. And I pray that you will do this because you have a sincere desire to spend more time listening to the Creator of the universe, enjoying the sound of his voice and the splendor of his presence.

So the first reason I wrote this book is to reverse the increasing trend of biblical illiteracy among Christians.

REASON #2

I also wonder whether Christians have forgotten *how* to read the Bible. When we do read the Word, it is my conviction we usually ignore the one Bible reading method that is most obvious and therefore most beneficial.

There are many edifying ways to read the Bible. But my experience tells me it is unlikely that you have ever read the Bible in the manner explained in this book.

After you've read this book, you will probably react the way I did when I first encountered The Forgotten Bible Reading Method. You'll be amazed and dumbfounded. You'll be saying, "How could I have overlooked this way to read the Bible for so many years? Why hasn't anyone told me about this before?"

This is the second reason I wrote this book: to teach Christians how to read the Bible in the manner that it was meant to be read. I'm determined to reverse the tide of ignorance concerning The Forgotten Bible Reading Method.

We have forgotten to read the Word. And we have forgotten *how* to read the Word.

My Christian friend, by the grace and power of God, may this book lead you to experience a new level of hunger for, understanding of and delight in God's truth as revealed in his matchless written Word.

And may time in the written Word bring you deeper intimacy with the living Word, our Lord and Savior Jesus Christ. May you see him on every page. And by seeing the living Word in the written Word, may you love, adore and obey him with greater degrees of understanding and passion all the days of your life.

WHY YOU SHOULD READ THIS BOOK

This is a book about a book about The Book.

"The Book" is the Bible.

"A book about The Book" is a 72-page book entitled "How To Master The English Bible" by James M. Gray, published in 1904 by The Bible Institute Colportage Association of Chicago.

Mr. Gray's book so revolutionized the way I read the Bible, I am now a man on a mission to present this work to anyone who seeks to understand the Word of God in all its glory.

If this "book about The Book" is so good, why don't I just recommend that you read "the real thing"? Well, believe it or not, Mr. Gray's book is out of print, although you can purchase a used copy at Amazon.com. And since it is in the public domain, you can also read it for free at websites like www.gutenberg.org.

But since it was written over 100 years ago, you might find it a difficult read, in light of the way our English language has changed. So my goal here is to explain the main points of Mr. Gray's book with a combination of paraphrasing and quoting. In addition, I've included "Questions for Reflection" at the end of each chapter that are designed to stimulate your thinking and are suitable for group discussion. I hope you find this approach understandable and beneficial :)

Of course, if you want to read the original, by all means, go for it! You'll find it here:

http://www.gutenberg.org/ebooks/41900

Before diving in, let's examine the foundational theological assumptions upon which this "book about a book about The Book" is based. The next chapter will explain why the Bible is the one and only indispensable source of divine truth that no person can live without.

CHAPTER 1. WHAT IS THE BIBLE?

THE BIBLE IS THE AUTHORITATIVE WORD OF GOD

"Who's In Control Here?"

On March 30, 1981 President Ronald Reagan was shot by John Hinckley. During the confusion to follow, Secretary of State Alexander Haig declared, "As of now, I am in control here in the White House," forgetting about the Constitutional line of succession. Some 25 years later, this historical footnote will appear amusing to some and inconsequential to others. To me, it is a parable of modern man's inability to understand and submit to the authority of God.

Who's in control? Who's in charge?

In charge of what? In charge of the universe? In charge of planet earth? In charge of our country, while the President's life hangs in the balance?

But for the grace of God, don't most of us miss out on the most important "control issue" of all: Who is in charge of my life?

Whether we realize it or not, we all live our lives under the authority of someone or something, don't we? And for many, we choose to be our own authority. That was my experience for many years - I loved being the captain of my ship and the master of my soul. I took pride in my personal freedom and cherished the thought of answering to no one but myself. Every day I would wake up and say to myself, "As of now, I am in control here of my life" . . . . thereby ignoring the authority of God and forfeiting the multitude of blessings promised to the one who submits to that authority.

The Bible both assumes and declares that God is the ultimate authority. From eternity past, He is the only one who can say, "I am in control here in this universe." Scripture repeatedly proclaims the sovereignty, lordship and kingship of God:

"The LORD reigns forever." (Psalm 9:7)

"The LORD is king forever and ever." (Psalm 10:16)

"You are enthroned as the Holy One." (Psalm 22:3)

"Dominion belongs to the LORD and he rules over the nations." (Psalm 22:28)

"The LORD sits enthroned over the flood; the LORD is enthroned as King forever." (Psalm 29:10)

So who's in control here? The Bible's answer is clear: God is. Whether we like it or not, whether we acknowledge it or not, whether we submit to it or not.

And the Sovereignty of God over all is inseparably linked to God's creation of all, His sustenance of all, and His ownership of all. God is in charge of all because He made it all, He sustains it all, and He owns it all. If you make something, don't you get to decide what to do with it? Don't you get to have total control over it and use it for your own purposes as you see fit?

The same is true of God. The Bible not only assumes and declares that God is the King of the universe, He is also the one and only Creator, Sustainer and Owner of the universe.

"Through him all things were made." (John 1:3)

"For by him all things were created . . . and in him all things hold together." (Colossians 1:16-17)

"The world is mine, and all that is in it." (Psalm 50:12)

"Everything in heaven and earth is yours. Yours, O LORD, is the kingdom; you are exalted as head over all. . . You are ruler of all things." (1 Chronicles 29:11-12)

"The God who made the world and everything in it is the Lord of heaven and earth . . . For in him we live and move and have our being." (Acts 17:24, 28)

Now comes a most amazing truth: This God, the Creator and Lord of all, has revealed Himself and His will to us through a written record known as the Bible.

The Bible declares itself to be the Word of God. When you open the Bible and read it, you are reading the very words of God because "All Scripture is God-breathed" (2 Timothy 3:16 NIV). The phrase "God-breathed", also translated "inspired by God" (NASB), means that it originates from God, comes from God or has its source in God. In other words, even though human writers were used by God to record the Bible, ultimately, Scripture claims that God wrote the Bible.

Since God wrote the Bible, and since God is the Sovereign Creator, Owner and King of all, then we must accept the authority of Scripture because it originates from the One who has absolute control over our lives.

This sequence of thought can be expressed in a syllogism of logic:

Premise #1: As Ruler of the universe, God has authority over my life.

Premise #2: God wrote the Bible.

Conclusion: Therefore, the Bible has authority over my life.

THE BIBLE IS THE INSPIRED WORD OF GOD

This phrase is a reference to the supernatural supervision of God over the human writers of Scripture so that the end result of their writing was the recording of the words that God wanted them to write.

"All Scripture is God-breathed and is useful for teaching, rebuking, correcting and training in righteousness, so that the man of God may be thoroughly equipped for every good   work."
(2 Timothy 3:16-17)

As mentioned above, the key phase in this passage is "God-breathed", also translated "inspired by God" (NASB). This phrase is not to be confused with our contemporary use of the word "inspiration", as in "I was inspired by that sermon to serve God wholeheartedly", or "I woke up this morning to a magnificent sunrise, and received the inspiration I needed to write a poem about the beauty of nature." We use the word to describe a sudden flash of intuition. We have an "ah hah!" experience and say, "I was inspired!" But the biblical concept of inspiration is a far cry from that.

Note that in 2 Timothy 3:16, it is the Scripture that is God-breathed, not the human writers. It is the Scripture that is inspired by God, not the human authors. This passage doesn't really address what the writers experienced personally when they wrote Scripture. Rather, the emphasis is on the Scripture itself -- the end result, the final product. And these written documents that Paul refers to as "Scripture" have their origin in God.

God miraculously supervised the writing of Scripture so that the message was recorded as He wanted it to be recorded. Truly this was a miracle; a divine process of communication from God to man occurred - and the resulting record is the very Word of God in written form.

So 2 Timothy 3:16 doesn't really tell us about the interaction between God and the writers of Scripture, because the writers are not even mentioned. To gain some insight into that interaction, we turn to 2 Peter 1:20-21:

"Above all, you must understand that no prophecy of Scripture came about by the prophet's own interpretation. For prophecy never had its origin in the will of man, but men spoke from God as they were carried along by the Holy Spirit."

Even though the human writers are mentioned here, again the emphasis is on the superhuman origin of Scripture. The prophet did not come up with this material - it did not come about "by the prophet's own interpretation." Its origin was not "the will of man", but came about as a result of these men being "carried along by the Holy Spirit."

"As a ship is empowered by and at the mercy of the wind, so also the writers of Scripture were totally dominated by God, here, in bringing the prophetic writings to others. Nothing that the Holy Spirit did not want to be inscribed ever was. And everything that He did want to appear, was written." (P.S. Karleen, The Handbook to Bible Study, New York: Oxford University Press, 1987.)

THE BIBLE IS THE PERFECT WORD OF GOD

Inspiration and inerrancy are inseparably linked. Because the Bible is inspired by God, it is therefore inerrant.

Inerrant means that the Bible is without error in the original manuscripts. It contains no mistakes or falsehood. It is perfect in every respect. Every word is true.

Follow the logic here: If the Bible is the Word of God, it must be inerrant, because God is perfectly righteous, full of truth and cannot lie.

"God is not a man, that he should lie." (Numbers 23:19)

"God, who does not lie." (Titus 1:2)

"It is impossible for God to lie." (Hebrews 6:18)

"He is the Rock, his works are perfect, and all his ways are just. A faithful God who does no wrong, upright and just is he." (Deuteronomy 32:4)

"Redeem me, O LORD, the God of truth." (Psalm 31:5)

Jesus said it quite plainly in his prayer to the Father on the night of his betrayal: "your word is truth." (John 17:17)

Paul commanded Timothy to correctly handle "the word of truth" (2 Timothy 2:15).

Since God wrote the Bible, and since God can only communicate truth, the Bible is completely true and therefore inerrant, that is, without error.

The inerrancy of Scripture is the clear testimony of Scripture:

"Your law is true." (Psalm 119:142)

"All your commands are true." (Psalm 119:151)

"All your words are true." (Psalm 119:160)

"The words of the LORD are flawless, like silver refined in a furnace of clay, purified seven times." (Psalm 12:6)

THE BIBLE IS THE ALL-SUFFICIENT WORD OF GOD

Peter wrote that "His divine power has given us everything we need for life and godliness through our knowledge of him who called us" (2 Peter 1:3). What a statement! What hope this gives us! We have everything we need for life and godliness - God has given us all we need to experience life as He intended it to be experienced and to live a life of godliness in accordance with His will.

And God has chosen to reveal His will for our lives through His written Word, the 66 books of the Bible. The Word of God, through the illuminating and empowering ministry of the Spirit of God, is sufficient to teach us everything we need to know to do everything for the glory of God (1 Corinthians 10:31).

Psalm 19:7-11 clearly states the sufficiency of Scripture. David uses several adjectives to describe the sufficiency of Scripture to meet the spiritual needs of man: perfect, trustworthy, right, radiant, pure, sure and righteous. And as such, when believed and obeyed, can accomplish the following: revive the soul, make wise the simple, give joy to the heart, give light to the eyes and provide great reward in both this life and the life to come.

The Bible contains a plethora of statements that collaborate the teaching of Psalm 19.

1. It revives the soul. To revive means to restore, refresh, convert or transform. The Bible contains the message we need to be transformed into Christlikeness! This is why Paul told Timothy that the Scriptures "are able to make you wise for salvation through faith in Christ Jesus" (2 Timothy 3:15). This is why Peter wrote the "you have been born again . . . through the enduring word of God" (1 Peter 1:23). So the Word of God has the power to transform a life through salvation and sanctification.

2. It makes wise the simple. To make wise means to become skilled in the art of godly living, the ability to make right choices to the glory of God. Psalm 119:98-100 is a compelling description of this: "Your commands make me wiser than my enemies . . . I have more insight than all my teachers, for I meditate on your statutes. I have more understanding than the elders, for I obey your precepts."

3. It gives joy to the heart. Again, Psalm 119 says it so well: "I rejoice in following your statutes as one rejoices in great riches. . . . I delight in your decrees (Psalm 119:14, 16). "Your statutes are my heritage forever; they are the joy of my heart" (Psalm 119:111).

4. It gives light to the eyes. The Scripture provides the light so desperately needed in our ever-increasing world of darkness. Solomon wrote: "For these commands are a lamp, this teaching is a light" (Proverbs 6:23). The Psalmist

the same truth: "Your word is a lamp to my feet and a light for my path" (Psalm 119:105).

5. It promises great rewards to the one who obeys it. Blessing will come to the man whose "delight is in the law of the LORD", to the man who meditates on the law day and night -- "whatever he does prospers" (Psalm 1:1-3). James reiterates this concept so clearly: "But the man who looks intently into the perfect law that gives freedom, and continues to do this, not forgetting what he has heard, but doing it - he will be blessed in what he does" (James 1:25-26).

The Bible is not just another good book. It claims to be the authoritative, inspired, inerrant and all-sufficient Word of God, and as such, our passion should be to read it diligently and prayerfully, asking the Spirit of God to illuminate our understanding of it and empower our obedience to it.

In light of all that Scripture says about it, shouldn't we dedicate ourselves to reading it and understanding it? Yet we have overlooked and even forgotten one of the best ways to do just that, as the next chapter will reveal.

CHAPTER 2. THE METHOD DISCOVERED

Like many Bible scholars, James M. Gray, president of Moody Bible Institute from 1904 to 1935, began full-time Christian service as a preacher. Before entering the world of Christian academia, he was pastor of the Reformed Episcopal Church in Boston for 16 years.

Amazingly, however, Mr. Gray makes this confession about his early years in the pastorate:

"For the first eight or ten years of my ministry, I did not know my English Bible as I should have known it, a fact to which my own spiritual life and the character of my pulpit ministrations bore depressing witness."

This man later spent 43 years at one of America's premiere evangelical Bible institutes, serving as summer guest lecturer, dean, executive secretary, editor of Moody Monthly magazine, president (for 31 years) and president emeritus. He authored 25 books and served as editor of one of the first reference Bibles ever published. Spanning parts of two centuries, his expositions of the Word blessed nearly 20,000 students.

And yet this is the man who spent at least eight years as a preacher who did not know the Bible as he should have known it. Is this not an incredible confession?

Fortunately, Mr. Gray realized this deficiency and decided to do something about it:

"My heart was greatly burdened in prayer about this for more than a year."

He was wise enough to recognize the problem, and he took the matter to God in prayer. Obviously this was causing him much concern and he was eager to find a solution.

I'll let Mr. Gray tell you how God answered his prayer in a very unexpected manner:

"My heart was greatly burdened in prayer about this for more than a year, when God answered me through a layman I met at a Christian convention. We were fellow-attendants at a certain Christian conference and thrown together a good deal for several days. I saw something in his Christian life to which I was a comparative stranger - a peace, a rest, a joy, a kind of spiritual poise I knew little about. I so much coveted his peace and joy in Christ, I asked him how he had obtained the blessing. He told me it came to him 'By reading the letter to the Ephesians.'

I was surprised, for I had read it without such results, and therefore asked him to explain the manner of his reading, when he related the following:

'I was going to spend a Sunday with my family in the country,' he said, 'and I carried with me a pocket copy of the letter to the Ephesians. In the afternoon I lay down under a tree and read it through at a single reading. My interest being awakened, I read it through again in the same way, and again, and again, as many as 12 or 15 times. When I arose, I was not only in possession of Ephesians, but Ephesians was in possession of me, and I had been lifted up to sit together in heavenly places in Christ Jesus.'"

And what was Mr. Gray's reaction to this man's account?

"I confess that as I listened to this simple recital my heart was going up in thanksgiving to God for answered prayer, the prayer really of months, if not years, that I might come to know how to master His Word. And yet, side by side with the thanksgiving was humiliation that I had not discovered so simple a principle before, which a boy of ten or twelve might have known. And to think than an 'ordained' minister must sit at the feet of a layman to learn the most important secret of his trade!"

QUESTIONS FOR REFLECTION

1. What was your reaction to Mr. Gray's confession that after serving as a Pastor for 8 years, he didn't really know the Bible "as I should have known it"?

2. Reality check: Evaluate yourself right now. Do you know the Bible as well as you should? Why or why not?

3. Here's a fascinating story of how "laymen" confounded the religious experts of their day. In Acts chapter 3, about 2 months after Jesus is killed, resurrected and taken up to heaven, Peter and John miraculously heal a 40-year old man who was crippled from birth. As a result of this healing and Peter's subsequent preaching of the gospel to those at the temple, about 2,000 people become Christians,

bringing the total number of male converts to 5,000 in Jerusalem.

Obviously, the Jewish religious leaders are quite upset about this. Hadn't they already gotten rid of this heretic named Jesus? (Known as "The Sanhedrin", this is the same group of men who condemned Jesus to death; see Mark 14:53-65, 15:1). Now his followers are causing a ruckus!

Let's pick up the story in Acts 4:1-12.

"The priests and the captain of the temple guard and the Sadducees came up to Peter and John while they were speaking to the people. They were greatly disturbed because the apostles were teaching the people and proclaiming in Jesus the resurrection of the dead. They seized Peter and John, and because it was evening, they put them in jail until the next day. But many who heard the message believed, and the number of men grew to about five thousand.

The next day the rulers, elders and teachers of the law met in Jerusalem. Annas the high priest was there, and so were Caiaphas, John, Alexander and the other men of the high priest's family. They had Peter and John brought before them and began to question them: "By what power or what name did you do this?"

Then Peter, filled with the Holy Spirit, said to them: "Rulers and elders of the people! If we are being called to account today for an act of kindness shown to a cripple and are asked how he was healed, then know this, you and all the people of Israel: It is by the name of Jesus Christ of

Nazareth, whom you crucified but whom God raised from the dead, that this man stands before you healed. He is " 'the stone you builders rejected, which has become the capstone. Salvation is found in no one else, for there is no other name under heaven given to men by which we must be saved."

Can you imagine what these religious leaders are thinking? The rulers, elders and teachers of the law are confronted by two men who have the power to heal and convince thousands to accept their message.

Yet note what Luke records next:

"When they saw the courage of Peter and John, and realized that they were unschooled, ordinary men, they were astonished and they took note that these men had been with Jesus." (Acts 4:13)

Peter and John were fisherman (Mark 1:16-20), not Old Testament scholars. They were "unschooled" and "ordinary" - in the minds of these Jewish religious leaders, they were "common folk" or "laymen". Yet who understood the truth and who was walking in the dark?

4. Compare the story of "the layman and the preacher" with the story of the apostles and the Sanhedrin. How are they similar? How are they different?

5. Reality check: Have you ever felt intimidated by other, more "knowledgeable" Christians who appeared to know the Bible better than you?

6. How has your perception of their apparent Bible knowledge affected the way you relate to them?

CHAPTER 3. THE METHOD TRIED

After hearing about the Bible reading experience of "the layman", Mr. Gray decided to give the method a try. Here's what he did:

"At once I began to apply this simple principle to the whole Bible, beginning at Genesis. I read Genesis through in the English at a single reading, and then repeated the process again and again until the book in its great outlines had practically become mine. Then I took up Exodus in the same way, Leviticus, Numbers and practically all the other books of the Old and New Testaments to Revelation, with the exception of Proverbs, the Psalms, and one or two others which do not lend themselves readily to that plan of reading.

I am careful to emphasize the fact that I did not read merely the Bible 'in course,' as it is commonly understood, but kept at each book until it was mastered before I began work in the next. One might read it in that way ('in course') a great many times and not master it in the sense indicated above. The plan was to read and reread each book by itself and in its order, as though there were no other book in existence, until each book had become a part of the very being."

So Mr. Gray started reading each book of the Bible repeatedly, in one sitting, until each book was mastered. He did not read the Bible "in course", which means to read Genesis once, then continue by reading Exodus once, and so on. Instead, he read each book multiple times in succession, and he did not proceed to the next book until he had mastered the current book.

Does that sound like a lot of reading? Of course!

Do you think it was worth it? I'll let Mr. Gray answer that question:

"Was the task tedious and long? No more than was Jacob's when he served Laban for his daughter Rachel. There were compensations all along the way and ever-increasing delight. No romance ever held sway over the thought and imagination in comparison with this Book of books. A better investment of time was never made by any minister; and shut me up today to a choice between all the ministerial lore I ever learned elsewhere and what was learned in this synthetic reading of the Bible, and it would not take me many minutes to decide in favor of the latter.

I cannot tell the effect upon me: strengthening my faith in the infallibility of the Bible, enlarging my mental vision, deepening my spiritual life, and lightening the burdens of my ministry. Words fail me to express the blessing that reading has been to me. "

QUESTIONS FOR REFLECTION

1. Mr. Gray claims that simply reading each book of the Bible multiple times paid enormous spiritual dividends: "there were compensations all along the way and ever-increasing delight". What is your reaction to this man's

testimony about the dramatic effect that God's Word had on his life and ministry?

2. Whether or not you have ever tried Mr. Gray's "synthetic reading" method, what benefits have you experienced over the years by reading the Bible?

3. Have you reflected lately on what the Bible claims to be? I'd like you to do so right now by reading Psalm 119, which is arguably the most descriptive passage in the Bible about the Bible - what it is, what it claims to be, and what benefits are offered to the one who cherishes it.

Go ahead and read Psalm 119 in one sitting - it's 176 verses long, but once you start reading it, I hope you'll find it difficult to stop! Read questions 4-6 below before you read Psalm 119, and while you are reading, have a pen and paper handy to jot down the answers to the following questions while you read.

4. What words (adjectives or nouns) and phrases are used to describe God's Word? Write them down. What benefits are promised to those who love, learn and obey God's law? (This list will be long . . . go for it!)

5. Take a look at your list from Question 4. Pretty impressive, isn't it? God's Word is righteous, wonderful, gracious, truthful, trustworthy, precious, eternal, sweet . . . It is a source of delight, freedom, comfort, understanding, wisdom, joy and peace. (Those are just a few of the characteristics of the Bible you should have found by reading Psalm 119.)

Now let's reflect on this awesome thought: virtually every one of these characteristics of God's Word are also used elsewhere in Scripture to describe God Himself! What does that tell us about the connection between God and His Word? What does this tell us about how we should go about getting to know God?

6. Do you know why I love repetition? Because God does! Go back and read the following verses in Psalm 119 - verses 24, 35, 47, 70, 77, 92, 143, 174. What word appears in every one of these verses (in the NIV)?

Now, read Psalm 37:4.

Comment on the relationship between finding your delight in God and finding your delight in God's Word.

Chapter 4. The Method Explained

Mr. Gray began to champion this approach to Bible reading and eventually wrote a book about it in 1904 called "How To Master The English Bible." He called this method "the synthetic study of the Bible." Why does he call it "synthetic"?

"The word 'synthesis' suggests the opposite idea to the word 'analysis'. When we analyze a subject we take it apart and consider it in its various elements, but when we 'synthesize' it, so to speak, we put it together and consider it as a whole.

Now the synthetic study of the Bible means, as nearly as possible, the study of the Bible as a whole, and the study of each book of the Bible as a whole, and the study of each book of the Bible in its relation to the other books."

In his book "How To Master The English Bible", Mr. Gray further expands this definition by outlining the following steps in the synthetic method:

STEP 1: Read The Book

"It is not asked that it be studied or memorized, or even sought to be understood at first; but simply read. The purpose is to make the task as easy, as natural, and as pleasant as possible. It matters not how rapidly you read it, if you but read it. But is it not strange that this is one of the last things many really earnest Christians and seekers after Bible truth are willing to do? They will read books about the Bible almost without limit, but to read the books of the Bible itself is another matter."

Take a trip to your local Christian bookstore and you'll find ample evidence that what Mr. Gray said in 1904 is still true today. The number of Christian books "about the Bible" (and any number of related topics) is truly "almost without limit." But how many Christians spend time simply reading the Bible.

STEP 2: READ IT CONTINUOUSLY

This stands for two things -- the reading of one book of the Bible uninfluenced by its divisions into chapters and verses, and the reading of one book of the Bible in its entirety at a single sitting.

"The chapter and verse divisions, it should be remembered, are of human origin and not divine, and, while effecting a good purpose in some particulars, are a hindrance to the mastery of the book in others. Sometimes a chapter or verse will cut a truth in half, whose halves state a different fact or teach a different doctrine from that intended by the whole, and necessarily affecting the conception of the outline."

Think about this for a moment: Did you realize that the chapter and verse designations of the Bible were not part of the original writing? They were added centuries later as a convenience for the reader. In other words, the chapter and verse designations are not inspired by God. There is nothing sacred about them, and as Mr. Gray so eloquently points out, they can actually cause the reader to misunderstand the meaning of a passage because we naturally (and sometimes incorrectly) assume that each chapter division, and to a lesser extent, each verse division, was intended by the writer to indicate a stopping point or a change in thought, when actually the writer of any particular book had nothing to do with those chapter/verse designations!

Now let's examine the phrase "in its entirety at a single sitting" Why is this so important? Because ...

"Many of the books of the Bible have a single thread running through the whole -- a pivotal idea around which all the subsidiary ones revolve -- and to catch this thread, to seize upon this idea, is absolutely necessary to unravel or break up the whole in its essential parts."

STEP 3: READ IT REPEATEDLY

The next rule is to read one book of the Bible repeatedly.

The old saying is so true: Repetition is a great teacher. Mr. Gray explains the importance of this concept:

"The reader will understand that by the 'book' in every case is meant the particular book of the Bible - Genesis, for example - which it is now being sought to master, and which is not to be laid aside for any other succeeding book of the Bible until the mastery is assured. This cannot usually be accomplished by one reading, but only by repeated readings after the manner designated."

STEP 4: READ IT INDEPENDENTLY

Next, read the book independently, that is, without the aid at first of any commentary, study guide, or any other Bible aids.

"These (books about the Bible) are invaluable in their place, of course, but in the mastery of the English Bible in the present sense, that place is not before but after one has gotten an outline of a given book for himself. Indeed, an imperfect or erroneous outline of one's own is better than a perfect outline of another.

The independent reading of a book in this sense is urged because of its development of one's own intellectual powers. To be ever leaning on help from others is like walking on stilts all one's life and never attempting to place one's feet on the ground.

Who can ever come to know the most direct and highest type of the teaching of the Holy Spirit in this way? Who can ever understand the most precious and thrilling experiences of spiritual illumination thus?

It is a great gain to so know the Bible for yourself that, carrying it with you wherever you go, you may be measurably independent of other books in its study and use."

STEP 5: READ IT PRAYERFULLY

Read it prayerfully, in reliance upon the Holy Spirit who inspired it to enlighten it to your understanding.

"The most important rule is the last. Let not the triteness of the observation belittle it, or all is lost. The point is insisted on, since the Bible is a supernatural book, it can be studied or mastered only by supernatural aid.

Coleridge said, 'The Bible without the Holy Spirit is a sundial by moonlight', and a greater than he said, 'We have received, not the Spirit of the world, but the Spirit which is of God, that we might know the things that are freely given us of God' (1 Corinthians 2:12)."

There you have it - a summary of Mr. Gray's Synthetic Method of Bible Reading.

Here are the five steps again:

1. Read the book.

2. Read it continuously, that is, in a single sitting, without observing its divisions into chapters and verses.

3. Read it repeatedly, until you have the consciousness of its possession in outline.

4. Read it independently, that is, without the aid at first of any commentary or other Bible study help.

5. Read it prayerfully, in reliance upon the Holy Spirit who inspired it to enlighten it to your understanding.

"The observance of these simple rules has never failed to produce the desired blessing."

QUESTIONS FOR REFLECTION

1. Reflect on your experiences as a Bible reader or Bible student. What Bible reading or Bible study methods have you used in the past? Share your thoughts: Which methods do you find enjoyable and why? Which methods did you dislike and why?

2. Have you ever heard of the "synthetic" Bible reading method? What is your initial reaction to it?

3. Based on what you know so far about the synthetic Bible reading method, are you willing to give this method a try? Why or why not?

Now that you have heard how Mr. Gray discovered, tried and explained this Bible reading method, let's unpack each of the five steps in more detail.

CHAPTER 5. WHAT ARE YOU READING TODAY? (STEP 1 UNPACKED)

Sometimes brevity is everything. When James M. Gray penned those three simple words, "Read The Book", I wonder if he realized how much power they contained.

Each of the five steps is indispensable to the successful implementation of the Synthetic Method. Yet at first glance, the first step may seem unnecessary or even an insult to one's intelligence. "Well, of course we have to read the Bible. That's what this is all about isn't it -- reading the Bible?"

Well, of course it is.

Then why did Mr. Gray include this step in the method? Why not get right to the "meat of the matter" and start with "Read it continuously" as Step 1?

I think Mr. Gray provides the answer to that question with this question:

"Is it not strange that reading the Bible is one of the last things many really earnest Christians and seekers after Bible truth are willing to do?"

And then he says something that just boggles my mind:

"They will read books about the Bible almost without limit, but to read the books of the Bible itself is another matter."

My friend, Mr. Gray made that comment in 1904. Is it not still true today? In fact, may it be even truer today than in 1904? Have you been to a Christian bookstore lately? Is there no end to the writing of books about every spiritual topic imaginable? And I'm thankful for the proliferation of good Bible teaching in print. Study guides, commentaries, topical studies, devotionals, biographies and autobiographies -- the number of Christian books, magazines and other printed resources is truly amazing.

But let's not sugarcoat Mr. Gray's point:

Dear Christian friend, did you read the Bible today?

Now I'm the first to admit that there are days when I do not read the Bible -- life happens, a child gets sick and your schedule is turned upside down, you go out-of-town and get out of the normal daily routine -- there are any number of legitimate reasons why you may not read God's Word on any particular day.

But on a consistent basis, do you read the Bible? Not just a book about the Bible, not a commentary or a Bible study guide, not a daily devotional that offers a single verse and few inspirational paragraphs -- I mean the Bible.

I believe this is Mr. Gray's point. Read The Book!

"But I just don't have time."

What would Mr. Gray say in response to that?

"We are living in a time when, if only for good form, we feel an obligation to be acquainted with the best authors. But shall we say that Shakespeare, or any other of the masters, is able to interest us in what he wrote, while He who created Shakespeare is unable to do so? Are we prepared to confess that God cannot write a book as capable of holding our attention as that of one of His creatures? What an indictment we are writing down against ourselves in saying that, and how it convinces us of sin!"

Strong words, don't you think?

And it again amazes me that these words, written in 1904, are still so applicable today. If you are a Christian but truly believe you do not have time to read the Word of God, what are you reading? And surely you are reading something, right? It may be the newspaper, a magazine, a "good book" -- whatever. Isn't Mr. Gray's analysis correct -- if you are not reading God's book, but are reading anything else, haven't you just indicted yourself?

Most people I know don't read Shakespeare, but don't we find any number of other contemporary authors that we are holding in higher esteem than the God who not only loved us so much that He sent His Son to provide salvation, but who also wrote a book to give us "everything we need for life and godliness"? (2 Peter 1:3)

Oh Christian friend, I urge you to not take the Word of God for granted. Take a moment today and reflect on what it is you are holding in your hand -- the very words of God!

QUESTIONS FOR REFLECTION

1. Reflect on your own attitude toward Bible reading in light of this comment: "Christians will read books about the Bible almost without limit, but to read the books of the Bible itself is another matter." Reality Check: Where are you at right now in relation to this comment? How do you assess your attitude re: reading the Bible vs. reading books about the Bible? Honestly, which would you rather do: read the Bible or read a book about the Bible?

2. Do you feel you are spending enough time reading the Bible? Why or why not?

3. If you see the need to increase your time in the Word, what do you need to do to make this happen? (change your schedule, wake up earlier, go to bed earlier, etc.) Be specific and be realistic.

CHAPTER 6. HOW WAS THE BIBLE MEANT TO BE READ? (STEP 2 UNPACKED)

When was the last time you received a letter in the mail? By a letter, I don't mean junk mail or your monthly bills, but a personal letter written to you by someone you know. Maybe a family member sent you one recently - your son wrote you from summer camp or your daughter sent one from college. Or a grandchild wrote you to tell all about his school field trip to the zoo.

Do you remember the anticipation you felt as you opened the letter and began to read? You couldn't read it fast enough, could you?

Now, stop and think about this: Did you read the letter in its entirety, or did you read only the first few sentences and put the letter down with the intent of finishing it later?

Perhaps you are thinking, "What a stupid question . . . Of course I read the whole thing!"

Now, stop and think about what happened some 2,000 years ago when the Christians living in Ephesus received a letter from the Apostle Paul. Do you think there was a buzz of excitement as these believers gathered around to hear what their spiritual father had to say to them? At the time this letter was written, Paul was imprisoned in Rome, but he kept in touch with the many churches he founded by writing letters - 13 of those letters have been preserved as part of Holy Scripture, and he undoubtedly penned many others that did not make it into the Bible.

Imagine being a Christian in first century Ephesus . . . when you come to the weekly prayer meeting at your neighbor's house, the elders are quite excited - "Paul sent us a letter! He's still in jail but he sent us a letter!"

So all the believers listen intently as the elder begins to read the letter:

"Paul, an apostle of Christ Jesus by the will of God, to the saints in Ephesus, the faithful in Christ Jesus: Grace and peace to you from God our Father and the Lord Jesus Christ."

The words just leap off the parchment and into your heart. Yes, that sounds like Paul all right. He called us "saints" and "the faithful in Christ Jesus." Oh, how sweet those words sound to your ears. It's like he's right there, in your midst, the words of truth flowing from his mouth with that unique combination of humility and boldness you came to love during the three years he spent in Ephesus as your spiritual leader.

The elder continues: "Praise be to the God and Father of our Lord Jesus Christ, who has blessed us in the heavenly realms with every spiritual blessing in Christ."

Yes! Yes! The believers all around you are now filled with joy. We have so many spiritual blessings in Jesus our Savior; we have so much to praise God for! Paul spent many hours explaining those blessings to us when he was here - oh, it will be great to hear him teach those truths again today through this letter!

But suddenly the elder stops and decides that is enough. "Come back tomorrow night and I'll pick it up where I left off. I don't want to read the whole letter tonight. That's all for now."

OK, you can quit pretending you are a first century Ephesian and come back to the 21st century. Perhaps my example above was a bit farfetched - you don't think the Ephesians would have read just the first few sentences of Paul's letter, do you? Of course not! They would have read the entire letter, right? They would have read the letter in its entirety -- in one sitting.

My friend, when was the last time you read one of Paul's letters in its entirety, in one sitting? Have you ever read any book of the Bible in its entirety, in one sitting?

Do you get the point? When Paul wrote his letters, they were written with the intention of being read -- in their entirety, in one sitting. So when we read Paul's letters, shouldn't we read them in the way they were intended to be read?

And couldn't we say the same thing about the other letters of the New Testament - those written by Peter, John, James and Jude? How about the four Gospel accounts and the book of Acts? (Most of the New Testament "books" were actually letters from the apostles, or a close associate of an apostle, to the first century Christians. Even the "books" of

Luke and Acts were written to an individual named Theophilus. See Luke 1:1-4 and Acts 1:1-2.)

And couldn't we say the same thing about virtually all the books of the Bible, both Old Testament and New Testament?

Sure, there are a few exceptions - as Mr. Gray pointed out, the Psalms and Proverbs come to mind, and some of the other Old Testament books may also not be suitable for reading in a single sitting - but when you think about reading the Bible, especially the New Testament books, are you starting to see value of the Synthetic Method?

From a literary standpoint, most of the books of the Bible, and certainly all the New Testament books, were written with the intention of being read in their entirety, in one sitting. To ignore this simple concept is to miss out on a depth of understanding that can only be realized when the Bible is read in the manner it was meant to be read.

Does that mean we should never take time to focus on an isolated verse or an individual passage? Of course not. Verse-by-verse, "take-it-apart-and-break-it-down-word-by-word" Bible study should also be a staple of the Christian spiritual diet. But for many Christians, this "passage a day keeps the devil away" mentality is the only type of personal Bible reading they know, and the bigger picture is never seen. Without the bird's eye view, the close-up picture will never capture all that God wants his children to learn from His Word.

To illustrate this point, consider this account of the synthetic method at work:

"In an address before the National Bible Society of Scotland, Dr. James Stalker spoke of the first time he ever read a whole book of the Bible straight through at a sitting. It was while as a student he was spending the winter in France, and there being no Protestant church in the town where he was passing a Sunday, he was thrown on his own resources.

Leaving the hotel where he was staying, he lay down on a green knoll and began reading here and there as it chanced, till, coming to the letter to the Romans, he read on and on through to the end.

'As I proceeded, he said, 'I began to catch the drift of Paul's thought; or rather, I was caught by it and drawn on. The mighty argument opened out and arose like a great work of art above me till at last it enclosed me within its perfect proportions. It was a revolutionary experience. I saw for the first time that a book of Scripture is a complete discussion of a single subject. I felt the force of the book as a whole, and I understood the different parts in the light of the whole as I had never understood them when reading them by themselves. Thus to master book after book is to fill the mind with the great thoughts of God."

Here's another example of the synthetic method in action:

"To read Genesis in this way (according to the synthetic method), will lead to the discovery that, large as the book is, it contains but five great or outline facts:

The history of creation

The history of the fall

The history of the flood

The history of the origin of the nations

The history of the patriarchs

It is then, a book of history, and the larger part of it is history of the biographical sort. This last-named fact (the history of the patriarchs), can be subdivided again into four facts:

The history of Abraham

The history of Isaac

The history of Jacob

The history of Joseph

And so the whole book can be kept in mind in a very practical way in eight words."

Once you've got the whole book of Genesis in your mind in this fashion, your understanding of the individual people and events of the book will be greatly enhanced."

QUESTIONS FOR REFLECTION

1. Have you ever read a single book of the Bible in its entirety, in one sitting? Share your experiences, if any - what book or books did you read, how long did it take, what effect did it have on you?

2. Reflect on Dr. Stalker's description of the first time he read a book of the Bible in its entirety, in one sitting: "It was a revolutionary experience. I saw for the first time that a book of Scripture is a complete discussion of a single subject. I felt the force of the book as a whole, and I understood the different parts in the light of the whole as I had never understood them when reading them by themselves. Thus to master book after book is to fill the mind with the great thoughts of God."

What are your thoughts on this "revolutionary" experience? Do you understand what he means, "I felt the force of the book as a whole"?

3. How about this comment: "I understood the different parts in the light of the whole as I had never understood them when reading them by themselves." What does that mean?

4. Do you have a desire to fill your mind with the great thoughts of God? Describe that desire.

Chapter 7. When Once Is Not Enough (Step 3 unpacked)

The third rule is to read one book of the Bible repeatedly. Mr. Gray writes:

"The reader will understand that by the 'book' in every case is meant the particular book of the Bible - Genesis, for example - which it is now being sought to master, and which is not to be laid aside for any other succeeding book of the Bible until the mastery is assured. This cannot usually be accomplished by one reading, but only by repeated readings after the manner designated."

Consider this analogy:

"A stranger sailing along the New England coast on a foggy morning could hardly believe there was a coast. But later, when the sun rises and the fog begins to dissipate, there is, at first, a line of sandy beach discernible, then a cluster or two of rocks, then a little vegetation, a house or two, a country road, the wooded hillside, until at last the whole of the beautiful landscape stands out in view.

It is much the same in the synthetic reading of a given book of the Bible.

The first view is not always satisfactory, and it requires a little courage to try again and again; but the effort brings a wonderful and inspiring result at last. The first reading of Genesis may not reveal what was spoken of above, but two or three readings will reveal it."

Perhaps you are wondering, "You mean I'm supposed to read one book of the Bible over and over again?"

Yes, that is precisely what Mr. Gray is suggesting.

"But that sounds so .... ummm.... redundant!"

Yes, of course it does. But let me ask you this: Have you ever tried it? Have you ever read any Bible book in its entirety, in a single reading, just once?

And most Christians, if they are honest, will say, "Well, uh, I guess not."

Then how can you be so sure that you will find this method to be redundant (or even boring, if that is the word you were tempted to use)?

At the risk of sounding like an old school marm, "Don't judge a Bible reading method by its cover!" I'm urging you to withhold judgment on this method until you've given it a fair chance to demonstrate its effectiveness.

Another common question is, "How many times should I read the same book?"

Remember the story of "the layman"? He read Ephesians about 12 or 15 times, and then what happened? - "Ephesians was in possession of me."

If this is your first attempt at the Synthetic Method, I suggest that you start out with an easier goal of 5 readings. Read the same book every day for 5 days in a row, and see what happens! After 5 days, if you want to continue with the same book, go for 5 more. After 10 days, you can then decide if you want to go for 5 more. I think 15 days is a good goal to shoot for, but if you don't make it to 15 days, that's OK. Your goal here is to master the book by getting the big picture -- and some people can master a book in fewer readings than others. See what works for you.

You can even give yourself a goal of reading that same book 5 times over a 7-day period, to allow for missing a day or two during the week.

"So I should read the same book for every day for 1 week, 2 weeks, even 3 weeks. What book should I read first?"

I think you should start with the shorter New Testament books -- by "shorter", I mean any book that is six chapters or less. There are 17 of them -- and each of these books can be read in its entirety, in a single sitting, in 20 to 30 minutes (or less):

Galatians
Ephesians
Philippians
Colossians
1 Thessalonians
2 Thessalonians
1 Timothy
2 Timothy
Titus
Philemon
James
1 Peter

2 Peter
1 John
2 John
3 John
Jude

In fact, some of these books can be read in 5 or 10 minutes. Philemon, 2 John, 3 John and Jude are only one chapter each!

So by starting out with these shorter books, I'm addressing the other most common question/objection about the synthetic method: "But I don't have the time to read an entire Bible book in one sitting."

And you already know how Mr. Gray would respond, don't you?

If you don't have 20 or 30 minutes to read the Bible, then do you really think you have a "time problem"? Might it be that you have a problem with your priorities? And as Mr. Gray did, might it also be time for you to go to God in prayer over this matter?

Here are a few other tips as you read the same book repeatedly:

1. Try reading aloud. This tends to dramatically improve both retention and understanding level.

2. Stick with the same Bible version/translation/paraphrase for at least 5 days. Then, if you like, switch to a different one.

3. Here's one of my favorite ways to read the Bible -- listen to an audio recording while you read along silently. Audio recordings of the Bible are abundantly available in tape, CD and MP3 format - check online at www.Amazon.com or at your local Christian bookstore.

For a free audio version of the World English Bible in downloadable MP3 format, visit http://www.audiotreasure.com/webindex.htm.

For a free audio version of the New International Version (New Testament only) for listening online via RealPlayer, visit

http://www.audio-bible.com/niv/

4. You can also listen to an audio recording while walking, driving, or doing other activities like housework, but I think you should "Read The Book" first! Be sure to read the book several times before you start to listen to it without the printed version in front of you. In other words, do not only listen to the book.

The goal here is to become so familiar with the book that it becomes a part of you. By exposing your mind to the book via different "entry points" (silent reading, reading aloud, silent reading while listening, only listening) you are increasing your retention level.

5. Woodroll Kroll of "Back To The Bible" has written an excellent book called "Read Your Bible One Book At A Time." This book is filled with valuable insights on the value of the Synthetic Method, along with estimated

reading times for all the books of the Bible. I love this book! It's subtitle is "A Refreshing Way to Read God's Word with New Insight and Meaning" - what a great description of the Synthetic Method.

Mr. Kroll has some challenging comments about this "I don't have enough time" issue:

"When you think about it, time really isn't the problem when it comes to reading the Bible. It's a good excuse, but not good enough. How much we read of the only book God ever wrote depends mostly on how much of it we want to read. Reading God's Word is less dependent on our schedule and more dependent on our desire and discipline."

You can get a copy of Mr. Kroll's book here:

http://www.amazon.com/Read-Your-Bible-Book-Time/dp/0830734783

QUESTIONS FOR REFLECTION

1. Reality Check: Is your desire to try the Synthetic Method starting to grow, or, while reading along so far, do you find yourself saying, "but I don't have the time!"

2. Were you aware that so many books of the Bible could be read completely in less than 30 minutes?

3. Reflect again on this analogy: "A stranger sailing along the New England coast on a foggy morning could hardly believe there was a coast. But later, when the sun rises and the fog begins to dissipate, there is, at first, a line of sandy beach discernible, then a cluster or two of rocks, then a little vegetation, a house or two, a country road, the wooded hillside, until at last the whole of the beautiful landscape stands out in view.

It is much the same in the synthetic reading of a given book of the Bible."

Does the importance of reading a book repeatedly make sense to you? Do you see why the old maxim "Repetition is a great teacher" is so critical to an adequate understanding of Scripture? Why or why not?

4. Does the idea of reading a book of the Bible 5, 10, 15, times appeal to you? Or do you find the idea redundant or even boring? Why or why not?

CHAPTER 8. FLY SOLO AT FIRST (STEP 4 UNPACKED)

The next rule is to read each book of the Bible independently, i.e. "independently, at first at least, of all commentaries and other outside aids."

"But I'm no Bible scholar! I need help to understand the Bible!"

I understand your point. And I appreciate your honesty and humility. Believe me, even Bible scholars need help to understand the Bible.

So let's start by noticing that 2-word phrase in the sentence above - did you catch it? You are to read each book of the Bible independently at first. Mr. Gray is not saying you should never consult an outside source. He is simply saying that you should wait awhile before you start reading outside sources. Start by reading just the Bible. Read it for yourself. See what you can understand on your own. Spread your spiritual wings and fly solo at first.

Obviously, Mr. Gray is not condemning commentaries or Bible study tools - he wrote many such books himself! He is the first to admit their worth: "These are invaluable in their place, of course . . ."

"But in the mastery of the English Bible in the present sense, that place is not before but after one has gotten an outline of a given book for himself. Indeed, an imperfect or erroneous outline of one's own is better than a perfect outline of another. The necessity to alter it when, by comparison, the error is discovered may prove a valuable discipline and education." ·

The above paragraph also sheds light on the question "How many times should I read a book?" Mr. Gray is suggesting that you read a book without outside help until you can formulate your own summary outline of the entire book. Don't worry that your outline is different than the one in your study Bible or commentary - it's your outline, and God will use it to help you get the big picture of a book on your own.

Mr. Gray shares two reasons for such independent Bible reading:

Reason #1: To Develop Your Study Skills

"The independent reading of a book in this sense is urged because of its development of one's own intellectual powers. To be ever leaning on help from others is like walking on stilts all one's life and never attempting to place one's feet on the ground. Who can ever come to know the most direct and highest type of the teaching of the Holy Spirit in this way? Who can ever understand the most precious and thrilling experiences of spiritual illumination thus? Should you wish to teach others, how could you communicate to them that sense of your own mastery of the subject so vital to a teacher had you never really dealt with it at first hand?

It is great to so know the Bible for yourself that, carrying it with you wherever you go, you may be measurably independent of other books in its study and use."

Reason #2: To Maintain Your Focus On The Big Picture

"But there is another reason for the independent reading of the book, and this is the deliverance from intellectual confusion which it secures. The temptation is, when an interpretative difficulty is reached, to turn at once to the commentary for light, which means so very often that the reader has become sidetracked for good, or rather bad, as the situation is now viewed.

The search for the solution of one little difficulty leads to searching for another, and that for another, until, to employ F.B. Meyer's figure, we have 'become so occupied with the shrubs and thickets of the landscape as to lose the conception of the whole sweep and extent of the panorama of truth.'

The 'intensive' has been pursued to the great disadvantage of the 'extensive', and usually there is nothing to be done but to begin all over again, for which every reader does not possess the required courage."

Have you ever been reading the Bible, come to a "problem verse", and then in your pursuit of the meaning of that one sentence, phrase or word, you lose sight of the overall meaning of the passage? This is a very common occurrence for Christians. It has happened to me many times.

You'll have plenty of time to chop down and examine every tree in the forest - later! For now, your focus must be on seeing the beauty of the whole forest. Don't get distracted by an exploration of the finer points. You are after the big picture, and it is critical that you never lose sight of this objective.

QUESTIONS FOR REFLECTION

Reflect on these comments:

You are to read each book of the Bible independently at first. Mr. Gray is not saying you should never consult an outside source. He is simply saying that you should wait awhile before you start reading outside sources. Start by reading just the Bible. Read it for yourself. See what you can understand on your own. Spread your spiritual wings and fly solo at first.

1. Right now, how dependent are you on outside sources (commentaries, Bible study guides, etc) when you read the Bible?

2. Well, what do you think about Step 4? Does the idea of reading the Bible without any outside help appeal to you, or does it intimidate you? Why?

3. If reading the Bible "on your own" is intimidating to you, are you ready to "cut the cord" and try a solo flight?

This section sheds light on the question "How many times should I read a book?" Mr. Gray is suggesting that you read a book without outside help until you can formulate your own summary outline of the entire book. Don't worry that your outline is different than the one in your study Bible or commentary - it's your outline, and God will use it to help you get the big picture of a book on your own.

4. Do you have any experience creating your own outline of a book (a Bible book or any other book)? Share your thoughts on those experiences.

5. Do you see the value in staying focused on the big picture and therefore ignoring "problem verses" until later? Or are you the kind of person who prefers to "understand everything" before you can move on. Explain.

CHAPTER 9. COME TO THE LIGHT (STEP 5 UNPACKED)

All five rules are indispensable. Yet Mr. Gray makes this statement about Step 5:

"The most important rule is the last." So please do not dismiss it or take it lightly: Read the book prayerfully.

"Let not the triteness of the observation belittle it, or all is lost. The point is insisted on because, since the Bible is a supernatural book, it can be studied or mastered only by supernatural aid.

Who is so well able to illuminate the pages of a given book as the author who composed it? How often when one has been reading Browning has he wished Browning were at his side to interpret Browning! But the Holy Spirit, by whom holy men of old wrote, dwells within the believer of Jesus Christ for the very purpose of bringing things to his remembrance and guiding him into all the truth.

Coleridge said, 'The Bible without the Holy Spirit is a sundial by moonlight,' and a greater than he said, 'We have received, not the spirit of the world, but the Spirit which is of God, that we might know the things that are freely given us of God' (1 Corinthians 2:12)."

How should we pray when reading the Bible? Scripture provides many prayers that I encourage you to make your own:

Every time you open the Word, pray as the psalmist prayed:

"Oh, how I love your law! I meditate on it all day long" (Psalm 119:97)

"Your word is a lamp to my feet and a light for my path" (Psalm 119:105)

"Open my eyes that I may see wonderful things in your law" (Psalm 119:18)

To receive illumination, you must come to the Light!

Before, during and after each Bible reading, pray the prayer of Paul for the Ephesians, that "the eyes of your heart may be enlightened in order that you may know the hope to which he has called you, the riches of his glorious inheritance in the saints, and his incomparably great power for us who believe" (Ephesians 1:18-19).

Take the words of Paul and personalize them: "Dear God, I ask you now to enlighten the eyes of my heart. I want to know the hope of eternal life; I want to know the riches of your glorious salvation; I want to know your incomparably great power for me, a believer. Please give me this knowledge through the reading of your Word. Amen."

QUESTIONS FOR REFLECTION

1. "Read the book prayfully. Let not the triteness of the observation belittle it, or all is lost." What do you think Mr. Gray means by the statement, "all is lost"?

2. "The Bible without the Holy Spirit is a sundial by moonlight." What does this mean?

3. How has the Holy Spirit illuminated your understanding of Scripture in the past? Or do you ever feel like reading the Bible is like taking a walk in the dark? Share your experiences.

CHAPTER 10. THE METHOD APPLIED TO 1 JOHN

Are you ready to try the Synthetic Method? Great! Here we go ...

Over the next 3 weeks, I'd like you to read the letter of 1 John about 15 times. This letter is 5 chapters long, and reading it should take you about 30 minutes, give or take a few minutes, depending on how fast a reader you are.

I'm suggesting that you read it 5 times each week rather than 7 times, to give yourself some slack and to remove the fear of "what if I miss a day!"

I'm going to give you some suggestions regarding what to look for when reading the letter. Of course, by doing this, we are breaking rule #4 (read independently), but this is a learning experience and I want to show you some general things to look for, not because I want to "teach you the book", but rather, to "teach you how to read the book." Sometimes having another person "show you the way" is the best way to learn.

So that is my objective -- to provide guidance as you pursue a Synthetic Reading of John's first epistle. You can then take what you learn and apply it to other books of the Bible.

WEEK 1:

Reading #1 -- Don't you love it when a writer tells you his purpose for writing? Some biblical writers do that, some don't. John does just that - in fact, he does it several times throughout the letter. Look for these "purpose statements", and as you read the letter, jot them down. After reading the letter, use these "purpose statements" to help you answer the question, "Why did John write this letter?" In your own words, paraphrase these verses into your own explanation of John's purpose(s) for writing.

Reading #2 - The last "purpose statement" (1 John 5:13) is viewed by many as the key verse of the letter. As you read, look for the many occurrences of the word "know" (and its various forms). How many times does this word appear in 1 John?

Reading #3 - Focus again on the key word "know". Write down all the things that John wants us to know. i.e. As you read, be asking yourself the question, "What does John want me to know?"

Reading #4 - Again, trace the concept of "knowledge" throughout the book. Now find the answer to the question: "How am I to obtain this knowledge?"

Reading #5 - Start to create your own "working" outline of the book. It doesn't have to be perfect, and don't worry about "getting it right". There really is no "perfect" outline. Just try to group verses together that address a common idea. And do not assume that the chapter divisions indicate a major change in John's thought progression. In fact, it is best to ignore the chapter divisions when creating an outline.

WEEK 2:

Reading #6 - John likes to describe a hypothetical situation in which someone "says" something or "claims" something. Take note of each of these verbal claims (there are 7 of them) - what is it that is being claimed? How do these claims relate to the purpose of the letter, and to John's frequent use of the word "know"?

Reading #7 - John uses a multitude of phrases to describe a Christian. As you read, jot down these phrases (there are at least 20 of them). How do these frequent descriptive phrases relate to the purpose of the letter? Examples of these phrases include: "have fellowship with him" (1:6); "come to know him" (2:3); "in him" (2:5); "in the light" (2:9), etc.

Reading #8 - In light of what you learned in Reading 6 and 7, reflect again on the purpose of the letter. Now what do you think is John's purpose in writing this letter? Has your understanding of John's purpose changed since Reading #1?

Reading #9 - Work on your outline in light of your findings in Readings 6, 7 and 8.

Reading #10 - Continue working on your outline.

WEEK 3:

Reading #11 - Have you tried reading aloud? If not, try it today.

Reading #12 - Read aloud again.

Reading #13 - Have you listened to an audio recording of the letter? If not, listen to it today while reading along silently.

Reading #14 - Listen to the audio without reading along silently.

Reading #15 - Have you gained any new insights as a result of reading aloud and/or audio listening? Make any additional changes to your outline in light of those insights.

CHAPTER 11. CONCLUDING THOUGHTS

Perhaps you are wondering, "Does anybody out there really read the Bible this way?" The answer is, "Yes!"

Here are 3 people I know who use the Synthetic Method.

1. John MacArthur

John MacArthur, well-known pastor, author and Bible teacher, embarked on a 3-year journey to better understand the New Testament. Here's what he has to say about the Synthetic Method.

"As a young guy in my early days in seminary, even a little bit before that, I was looking for a way to understand the New Testament better and I found a way to do that by repetitiously reading it. I read an old book, How To Master The English Bible by James M. Gray, an early president of Moody Bible Institute who suggested that if you wanted to retain the Bible, you had to read it repetitiously and not just read it once and keep moving.

And so, I decided that what I'd do is read every book of the Bible . . . break it down into sections that were manageable and I would do that for 30 days. Then I figured at the end of 30 days I would pretty well have in mind what was in that portion of Scripture.

And I started with 1 John and it was brief, only five chapters, so I decided I'd read it every day for 30 days. At the end of 30 days I felt like I still didn't quite have it all so I said I'll go 60 days. At the end of 60 days I said I don't think

I've got it yet and I went 90 days. And so every day for 90 days I read 1 John until it became very familiar to me.

. . . . By the way, I did eventually finish the New Testament, it's about a two and a half, three-year process to do that but you have to stick with the 30 days and not do 90 or it will elongate the whole process."

(Source: "Live By A New Love", sermon delivered October 6, 2002 at Grace Community Church. http://www.gty.org/resources/sermons/62-13/live-by-a-new-love)

2. As mentioned earlier, Woodrow Krull has written a book called "Read Your Bible One Book At A Time." This book is filled with valuable insights on the value of the Synthetic Method, along with estimated reading times for all the books of the Bible.

You can get a copy of Mr. Kroll's book here:

http://www.amazon.com/Read-Your-Bible-Book-Time/dp/0830734783

3. Me (the author)

I first heard about Mr. Gray's book and the Synthetic Method in 2005 while listening to John MacArthur's sermon mentioned above. I was intrigued by the concept, so I tracked down a copy of "How to Master the English Bible" and read it. I then started reading the shorter books of the New Testament repeatedly, in one sitting.

I started with Ephesians, and I remember reading it about 15 times over a 3 week period. I was blown away by the impact it had on my understanding. It really worked!

I've continued to read the shorter New Testament books in this manner, off and on, for the past several years. There are many ways to read the Bible, and this is not the only way that I read the Word, but every time I read a particular book repeatedly in one sitting, I am greatly blessed :)

So I urge you with all my heart to try it for yourself. And please feel free to contact me and let me know how it goes! You can reach me at GodWroteTheBook@gmail.com

Thank you for taking time to read this book about a book about The Book.

ABOUT THE AUTHOR

WAYNE DAVIES lives in Fort Wayne, Indiana with his wife and three children. He is a graduate of Grace College (B.A. in Biblical Studies) and Columbia International University (M.A. in Theology).

Wayne is President of Good Messengers Ministries of Fort Wayne, an evangelical ministry dedicated to equipping Christians to communicate the Biblical gospel. For more information, visit www.Good-Messengers.com.

Looking for more Bible reading tips? For a free copy of Wayne's Resource Guide, "Top 5 Free Online Bible Study Tools", visit www.GodWroteTheBook.com

For more information about Wayne's books, please visit www.GodWroteTheBook.com/books

You are welcome to contact Wayne directly with your comments or questions at GodWroteTheBook@gmail.com

ONE LAST THING...

If you enjoyed this book or found it useful I'd be very grateful if you'd post a short review on Amazon. Your support really does make a difference and I read all the reviews personally so I can get your feedback and make this book even better.

If you'd like to leave a review please visit this book's page on Amazon and scroll down to "Customer Reviews." Here's the link . . .

www.amazon.com/dp/B00SEDLVH6

Thanks again for your support!

Made in the USA
Coppell, TX
20 May 2023